Text copyright © 2025 by Sarah M. White.
Illustrations copyright © 2025 by Tessa Gibbs.

All rights reserved. No part of this book may be
reproduced in any form without written
permission from the publisher.

Library of Congress Cataloging-in-Publication Data available.
ISBN: 978-1-68555-777-5
Ebook ISBN: 978-1-68555-994-6
LCCN: 2024913077

Manufactured in China.

Printed using Forest Stewardship Council®
certified stock from sustainably managed forests.

10 9 8 7 6 5 4 3 2 1

The Collective Book Studio®
Oakland, California
www.thecollectivebook.studio

Our Food Grows

Written by Sarah M. White

Illustrated by Tessa Gibbs

Did you know our food grows?

We buy our food in grocery stores . . .

. . . but many foods grow from plants.

Strawberries

Strawberries grow close to the ground.

Their seeds sparkle on the outside.

Tomatoes

Tomatoes grow on climbing vines.

Asparagus

Unpicked asparagus grow into ferns.

The shoot is what we eat.

Peas

Peas grow inside a pod.

Each pea is a seed for a new plant.

Corn grows on a tall stalk.

One piece is called a kernel.

Which one brings a smile to your plate?